Memory's Junkyard

The Light We Kept

Elizabeth Berry

India | USA | UK

Copyright © Elizabeth Berry
All Rights Reserved.

This book has been self-published with all reasonable efforts taken to make the material error-free by the author. No part of this book shall be used, reproduced in any manner whatsoever without written permission from the author, except in the case of brief quotations embodied in critical articles and reviews.

The Author of this book is solely responsible and liable for its content including but not limited to the views, representations, descriptions, statements, information, opinions, and references ["Content"]. The Content of this book shall not constitute or be construed or deemed to reflect the opinion or expression of the Publisher or Editor. Neither the Publisher nor Editor endorse or approve the Content of this book or guarantee the reliability, accuracy, or completeness of the Content published herein and do not make any representations or warranties of any kind, express or implied, including but not limited to the implied warranties of merchantability, fitness for a particular purpose.

The Publisher and Editor shall not be liable whatsoever...

Made with ❤ on the BookLeaf Publishing Platform
www.bookleafpub.in
www.bookleafpub.com

Dedication

For my friend—
all things serve the Beam.
Even disco pirate buffalo.

Preface

I don't know how to start this book without admitting that I never know how to start anything. My mind is a crowded attic of half-finished projects and emotional souvenirs. So here we are, standing knee-deep in the junk, looking for what still works.

If these pages do anything, I hope they remind you that not everything needs to be shiny or new to matter. Sometimes the most meaningful things are the ones we almost threw away.

Acknowledgements

Doug
For always knowing when to hand me a snack, a capo, or a reason to keep going.
For the endless drives, the late-night laughter, and the gentle reminders that life is bigger than the bad days.
You're the constant hum beneath every song I love.

My Creative Family
For the ones who keep the lamp burning when the dark gets loud.
For those who prove that sincerity is still punk rock.
For the makers of noise and meaning, kindness and chaos.
For the ones who build beauty out of the wreckage, again and again.

You are the light we kept.

And to anyone who ever made something just to survive—welcome home.

1. Blade

From Abilene High's literary magazine, the Aquila, 1998

-

My life is balanced
on the edge of

his knife.

Everything —
my whole life —
comes down to this.

The pocket knife
in my hand.

Choices must be made.

Will the knife be sheathed
for one more night?

I know not...

I must keep
my hands moving,
keep busy —

because there's the blade,
waiting for me.

My own personal
Sword of Damocles.

Oh God,
do not still my hands...

Speed is life.

But I don't know
how much more
I can take.

2. Call Out

(1998)

I call out —
no one hears me.

Echoes come back,
taunting perfect clarity.

I built a fire
to warm me,
to keep out the dark.

Burning.
Burning.

The sky —

LOOK!

The moon is crimson.

A smile touches wary lips.
I'm going home.

3. Lizard King

(1998)

Lizard.
Leather.
Black Death.
Demon.

Human — he screamed
for a living.
(*Wouldn't we all if the money was good?*)

And he shocked them,
for they were too easy to shock.
And he was bored,
because it would take future generations
to mix and breed
to produce the kindred of his spirit.

When now he is nothing
but a floating phantom.

Death came at long last.
He is known because he did what no one else
(have)
had courage to do.

And courage is enviable.
And he had the soul of a poetic
clown.

Death smiled,
and he joined the club.
But is he happy now?

4. In Keeping With Dates

(1998)

April 8th
Friday.
My best friend's birthday.

Driven home in disbelief,
staring at Kurt —
no, not Kurt,
another different Kurt —
telling me the news.

News of death
at the hands of
miscarried fame
and a suck on a double-barrel.

The screaming poet is dead,
and a part of me screamed.

A part that died
with its awakening,
for it loved him.
And then,
so too did I.

They honored him,
and showed his better days
at the top of every hour.

And I saw pain in his face —
and I had to look away,
because I saw something.

Recognition.

I saw the face of myself,
and a thousand others,
burning anguished candles.

And his young widow-bride,
cursing the club,
and the bright eyes —
bright, cursed eyes —
of his daughter.

What does the future hold for her?
(for us all?)

5. The Kids Who Lived

It's not a phase, Mom.
My polish is just as chipped
at forty-four
as it was at fourteen.

I still pore over the sleeves,
the lyrics,
like I did then.
Now—
I know and love the
hands and hearts who wrote it.

It's a shame
we never love as fiercely
as we did back then.

We never knew what
hurt was
until it was too late.

The stars streaking the sky,
falling to earth,
aren't as bright as they
were back then.

But we make do.
We line our eyes
just a little too heavy.

We play music in the office
parking lots
just a little too loud.

We still wear combat boots
to the business-suit combat
of daily lives.
It means just as much as it
did then.

We just hide raw hearts
behind the barbed wire of
experience.

But we lived.
We stayed.

No one howled from heartsickness

for us.
Yet.

6. Home Was the After

What is home?
If you return
and are refused,
it was never home.

Certainly not a missing year,
notes taped to lampshade crenellations —
Gone to so-and-so's
(future ex-husband).
Don't wait up.
She never did.

The only port
in a storm
I didn't create.

Will this affect me?
No.
The bald-faced lie
sunk between us

like a spent mortar shell.

Home waited decades down the road.
Lessons learned,
ill-fitting relationships
shed like garments.

You will know home
because it can't be bought,
or stolen.

I built it myself
out of cat hair and bones,
guitar picks,
eyeball bouquets,
and the kind of friends
I would die for.

An impeccable —
(impervious) —
credit score
you can pry
from my cold,
dead fingers.

I will make all
the best decisions

because you never did.

I will win,
because my love never hurt.
My love never stole
safety,
security,
sanity.

I never forced choice.
My love never
sacrificed innocence
on its altar.

Fake home façade,
barely remembered —
I owe you nothing.

Heartless?
I learned
what I never, ever, ever want to be
from the best.

7. Memory's Junkyard

Is there a gaslight class?
So I can do it myself?
You think I *want*
these memories?

I remember every
unkind thing—
every word
spoken in anger.

Every attempt
at lessening
the self
of your *other*.

Ask me why
I can't stop.
Ask me why I
console myself now
with ten of everything

you took away.

Memory's junk yard—
building a
mind-body-spirit
hoard.

Feel better?
Feel... safe?
Still.
Waiting.

8. I Loved You, I Loved It All

Flooding is so last season.
No one floods anymore.

Antediluvian.
Denouement.

All the hip deities use fire—
it's so
HOT.

Global warming.
Climate change.
(A nuclear winter feels warm.)

How about an asteroid?
It was good enough
for the dinosaurs.

It's a surprise.
Where would you choose to be?

(5
more
minutes.)

How would you spend
your sands
through the humanity glass?

Big spoon,
little spoon,
like the old couple in
Big Boat, Iceberg.

(Manic panic.)

Will my companions
seek hands for comfort—
or hide under the bed?

I always said,
"Bury me in the backyard."
Who knew I'd see out that scenario?

Not a bang.
Not even a whimper.

I loved you.

I loved it all.
Never forget.

Balloon hiss.
Leak.
Silence.

9. Blink

Give me something
to eat.

I'll make a meal
from one word—
punctuation,
or lack thereof.

Weaned on
silence = threat.

Purse-lipped.
Eggshells.
Muscle-twitch jawline,
coiled for
bear trap spring.

Are you mad
at me?
I didn't do anything.

Analyze every word,
every deed,
for suitability
and consumption.

Can't I just blink?
Breathe in and out?
Why does it have to mean something?

10. Day One

No honor amongst thieves.
No loyalty to dragons.

Arcane and useless,
I speak the wrong tongue
to be useful.
Helpful.
Trapped.

Gray-haired bureaucracy—
let out now,
on parole.
Institutionalized.

The world:
unrecognizable.
Big.
Loud.
Full of hate.

Brooks was here.
And so was I.

No marks made
as progress is erased.

Send us a sign.
(*scream*)
No one listens.

11. Jesus of Cats

Jesus of cats,
take the wheel.

From this—
thy tiny crumpled figure,
eyes shut,
every ragged gasp
agony.

This patch of pavement?
Mine.

All I can hear is terror.
Too tired to fight.

Head droops.
Hands scoop.
Sweet voice.
Forehead kiss.

Retching sound.
Reek of death—
pungent in the air.

(What do we say?
Not today, Mister Death!)

Sweet voice.
Kind hands.
Eyes finally open.
Pain recedes.

Breaths rasped
are still breath—
life.

I repay
first-felt kindness
with pink-leopard-bandaged
paw biscuits—
a king's ransom
for hope-to-be,
bosom companions.

I'll be good.
Promise—
you'll see.

12. The Weak Pulse of Containment

One star.
Would not recommend.

That no man
is an island—
blissful
in societal containment.

Exclusion.
Punch holes in the lid
for breath.

It doesn't flutter.
It doesn't move.
A weak pulse.
A canned audience gasp.

Dead on arrival.

Please—
leave me alone.

I should have grown up
(died)
thirty years ago.

13. Terrible Freedom

Cosplay as someone
you might like.

Sometimes I even
fool myself.

Dysmorphic mirror gaze.
Funhouse reflection.
Mile-wide hips,
no matter the angle.

Carnival glass.
Ass.
Simple.
Dimple.

Patchwork-color quilt skin
that will never be thin.

Terrible freedom in

letting go—
giving up.

Fat girls
with the tragically pretty faces.

14. The Compliment Bar

Your name is a song
I hum
when silence feels too loud.

I was born with music—
it just belongs to someone else.

Tell me what
you would have me hear
to drown out the *me* voice
that isn't real.

Internal monologue
when the author
isn't even a fan
of my work.

I'm so glad
the main character survived.

You set the compliment bar
unattainably high—
without even trying.

Heaven help
the one you love.
Indeed.

Cat Stevens beard.
Dark glasses.
A soul hidden
because it doesn't know
what to become yet.

15. You Don't Love Me

You don't love me.
If you did,
I would know.

It would be loud—
dramatic—
sharp around the edges,
or a sucker-punch of quiet
(just like Mom
used to make).

You gas up my car.
No scorn.
No glare.
You tie my shoelaces
when my back hurts
so bad
I can't breathe.

"You don't love me!"

He doesn't hear me.
He's working in the yard,
tending my monsters—
both evident and not so.

If I was nicer
you wouldn't recognize me.
Obviously there is
something unspeakable
in the raw,
unlovely,
unloved me.

Or else,
why does everyone run?

I dress in self-protection
and pin on the label:
"Sarcasm is how I hug."

Must adore my spikes,
weakness,
vulnerability—
all for someone else.

For one not embraced
in stony silence,

then demolished
by Pandora's box.

The world's only horror?
Bites of reality.

Love only destroys.

You don't love me.
You can't.
You're. Still. Here.

16. A Fragment of Yesterday

I found a fragment of yesterday
tucked in the corner of the room.

Wasn't even a day worth remembering—
but I'll save it just the same.

I was where I wished to be.
Chickens pecked and scratched
in the dirt
outside my window.

Cats were available for petting.

My favorite blanket —
soft —
pulled up to my chin,
for no other reason
than it pleased me to do so.

Sleep came and went

as the day's light
crawled through the curtains,
up my toes,
across my body.

I missed huge swaths
of plot
in the name of somnolent
comfort.

You were there too.
No choices were made.
No decisions spoiled
the quality of dust motes
in the air.

I will place the fragment
on my special shelf
with all the others.

17. Sold to Chaos' Agent

We carry our ghosts
in pockets sewn too tight.
Jeans lack the means.
Watch pocket resolution.

Ripped bodice.
Fink fake.
Lies and ruffles
drip down throat-back—
I don't want to know.

Con gonna be fiction.
Suckerfied.
Surf and turf.
What are ya gonna do?
Sold to chaos' agent.

Answer the question.
Come out,
come out,

whatever you are.

You have to pay.

Natural qualities.
Inherent lack.
Cruelty.

18. Guest of Honor

Clap your hands
if you believe.

Fairy dust
and enough happy—
(Special K)
complete breakfast thoughts
to skid along
above the ground.

Emotionally impermanent.
Not quite flight.

Quick—tell me any of this mattered.
Tell me any of this
made a difference.

Quick—before I blink out,
extinguish like a candle.

Who watches
the watchers?
No one.

Soon—everyone eats fried chicken
at the potluck,
gets up,
leaves.

Except you—
guest of honor.

One day there will be
the room everyone else gets to leave
but you.

Open a window
lest you circle the ceiling,
bumping your head.

19. Emotional Obsolescence

I have stitched together
every silence left behind.

A quilt of betrayal
offers no warmth.

Time passes.
It goes in a drawer—
marked for special,
forgotten
introspection.

When is a hurt,
like hands around a throat,
ever convenient?

Still—
I take it out,
examine it
from all angles.

Like the questions
with no answers.

Why are some couplings
ambrosia to the soul,
while others offer
only shriveling poison?

Why will she vacuum
for him?
Menial chores
with a blank plaster smile.

Why does the new family
love their patriarch
when his hands (and heart)
only ever itched
to hurt—
hurt me?

Why do we examine
ancient scars?
Pale tissue holds
barely enough reminder.

Emotional obsolescence.

Still—
you never forget
your first.

20. The Light You Carry

I rely on you
to be okay—
watch your smile
throughout my day.

Feel your warmth
through daily strife;
count improved
my weary life.

I try to smile,
sometimes I fail—
grey office space
feels like a jail.

But there you are,
truthful light-bringer;
I count myself lucky—
my friend, my singer.

21. I Was Here

Born too late
to spin the platters that mattered.

Now I'm just a voice
in a sea of millions,
all screaming:

See me.

Give me what I never had —
a place to belong.

A Looney Tunes,
people-shaped hole in the wall,
or the door —

I was here, before.

No one noticed
but the Light Bringer,

the Truth Teller,
and his thrice-spliced knight.

Word-slingers,
hearts cracked
by too much frantic,
frenetic rocking.

Please —
don't let the lights go out.

Too much time.
Not enough to do.
(*Scratch that. Reverse it.*)

See you later,
bouncing baby girl,
paid for with an alligator song.

Disco buffalo.
Laser gun.
Slo-mo off a cliff(f).

Come back later.
Some other day.

Mr. Death(ray), we need our friend.

You can bend him right down the middle —
but never break.

Chicks dig scars.
Each one a (tower) story.

Healed once
by a storyteller's hand —
the same hand
that built worlds
and saved the broken things
inside them.